Ostrich MgQuarck is the Worst Detective in the World

a (Twitter-sized) novel

of murder & intrigue

by Liam Leroux

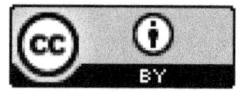

Created with the help of Edmonton Public Library

Published by Postcard Press Publishing Co.

2017

Prologue:

The World's Worst Detective

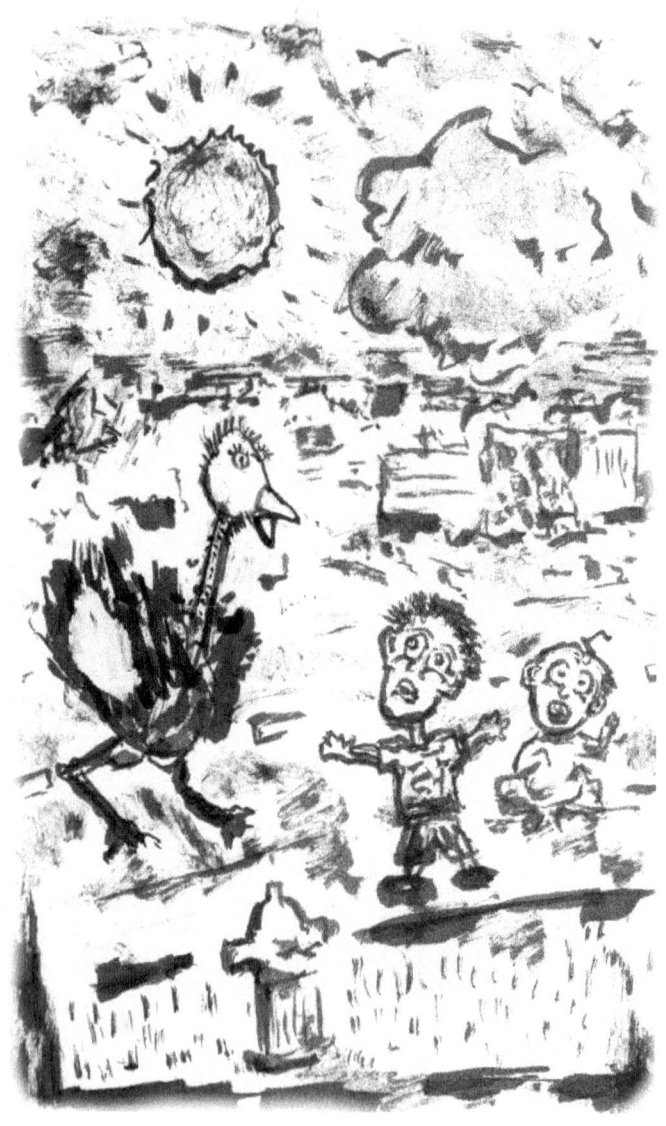

His name is Ostrich MgQuarck and he is the worst detective in the whole world.

MgQuarck doesn't like being the worst detective in the world, he doesn't even like being an ostrich but, with a name like "MgQuarck", his career was inevitable.

Obviously, ostriches are terrible detectives. Ostriches can't speak or understand any human languages, which means interrogating suspects is especially difficult.

Also, because he is an ostrich, most people assume he isn't smart. All of these people are correct. An ostrich is a large flightless bird capable of running with great speed across a savannah but incapable of logic, reasoning, or rigorous scientific analysis, which are all necessary qualities for any self-respecting detective.

Luckily for MgQuarck most is not all and he finds just enough business to survive.*

---

* Important note for potential clients of an ostrich detective. There is a common but incorrect myth regarding the position of the ostrich head during moments of crisis or danger. An ostrich will not bury its head in the sand when frightened, it will merely run away, or slice you to ribbons with razor sharp claws. Which, to be fair, is still terrible behavior for a detective.

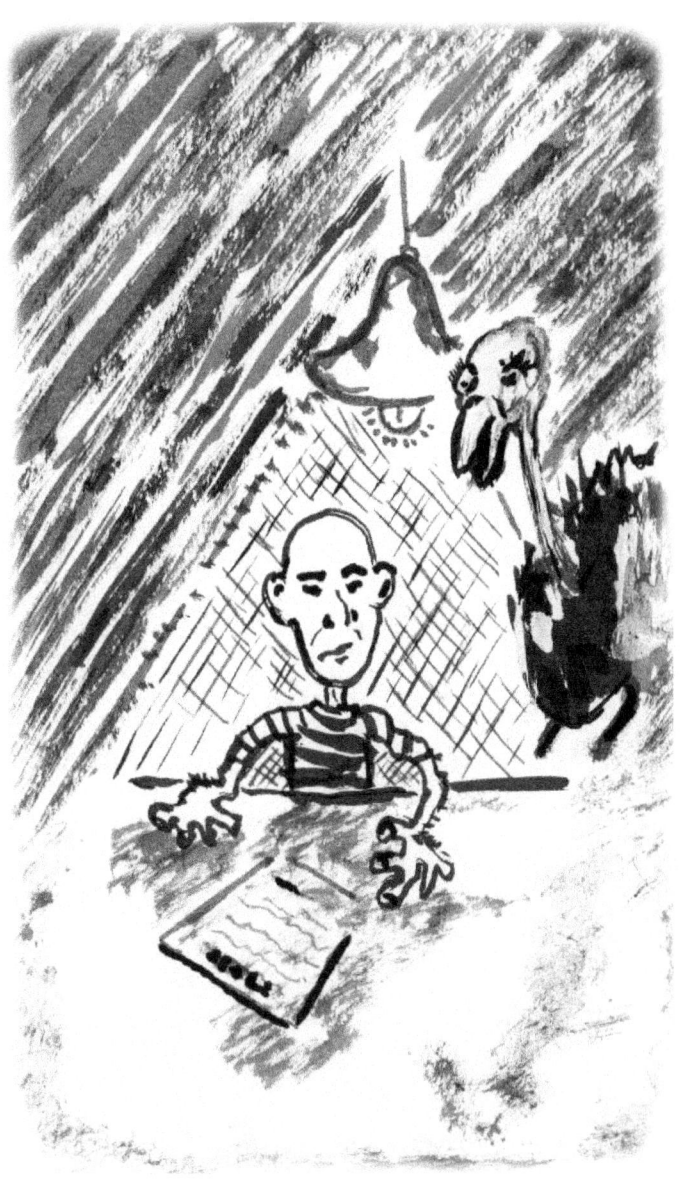

CHAPTER 1:

The Curious Case of

the Cuckolded Husband

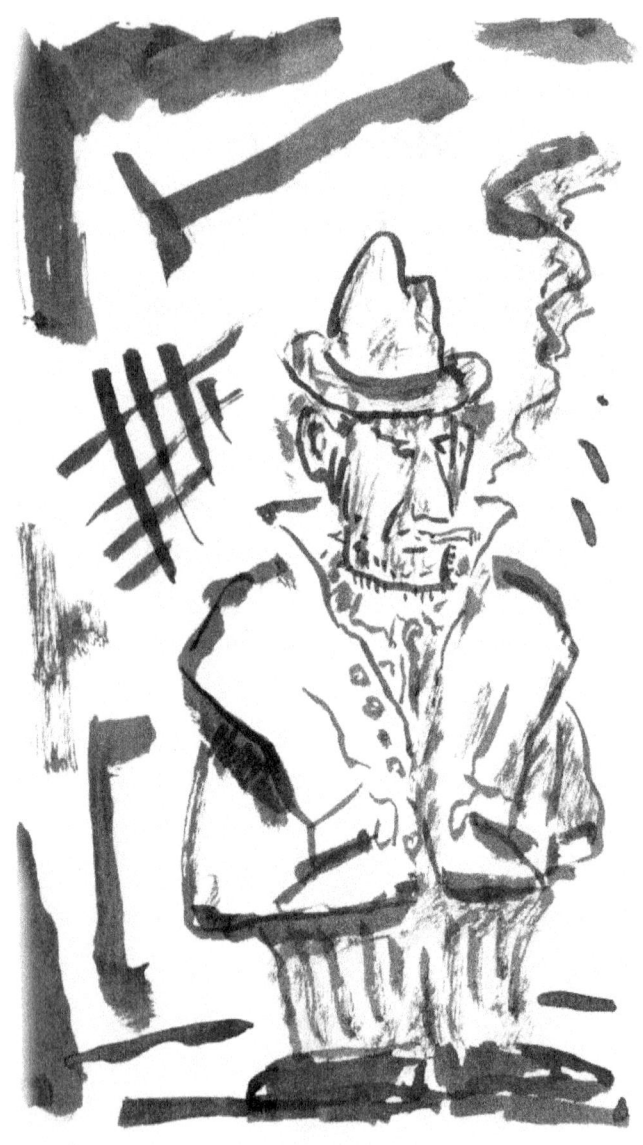

- Lieutenant Jorgensen, what's the situation here?

- Well chief, it's like this. There are two dead bodies in the bed upstairs, one male and one female. The dead man in the bed is not the same person as the man pictured in the wedding photographs hanging in frames on the wall. Seems a pretty straightforward case of a cuckolded husband pushed over the edge.

- Lieutenant you're dead right. This case is much too complicated. We need Ostrich MgQuarck.

- What? No! I didn't say that at all.

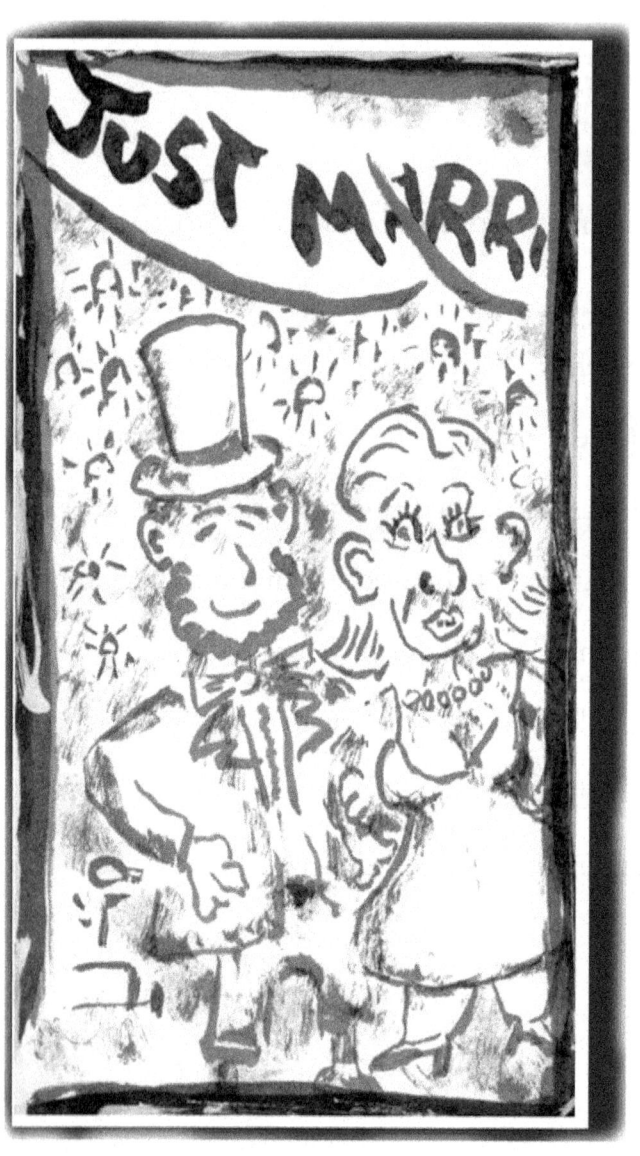

- Sergeant?

- Yes chief?

- Get MgQuarck down here right away.

- But chief, MgQuarck is the worst detective in the world.

- Keep an open mind here Lieutenant, MgQuarck might be our only chance.

- No! No he's not. He's an ostrich! What the hell are you thinking?

- Sir? MgQuarck is here. He's outside in the police van.

- Excellent. Gather round men, it's time to watch the world's finest detective in action.

- This is completely retarded.

- Quiet Jorgensen. Ok sergeant, open the van.

- Crikey chief! Look at him run.

- Quick men, follow him. He's already got a lead.

- Look, he's gone straight into the bar at the end of the road.

- Hey, what's going on here? What's with all the cops? And why the blazes is there an ostrich in my bar?

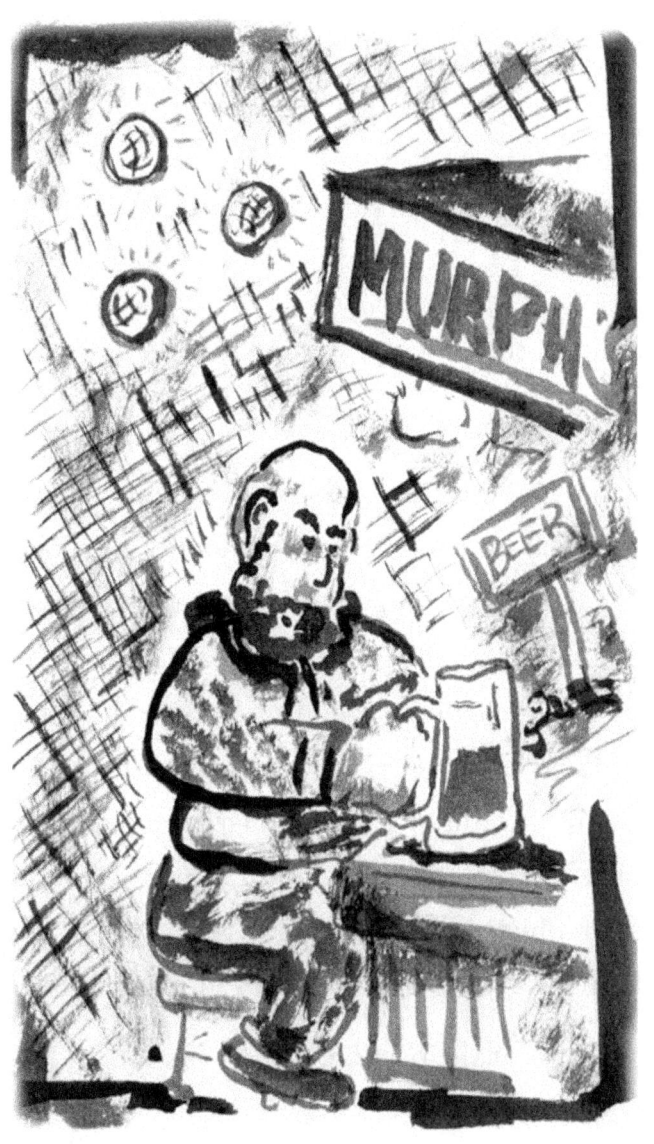

-This is Ostrich MgQuarck, the finest detective the world has ever known.

- That's the stupidest thing I've ever heard.

- He's hot on the trail of a wanted killer.

- Hi, that's me. I wanted one last beer before coming to turn myself in. I should have done it years ago. She had one affair after another and laughed at me when I asked for a divorce. Her father owns a money-tree factory. They genetically engineer trees to grow money leaves. I knew I'd never get away with it but I had the satisfaction of seeing the look on her face, just before I pulled the trigger. I told her I didn't buy the gun for shooting rabbits! AHAHAHAHHAHA.
 HAHhahahe… cough, cool. Ok, I'm ready to go now. Thanks for the beer barkeep.

- MgQuarck! You've done it again.

- No! He didn't do anything. He just ran out of the van in a straight line, directly into the bar. It was a jealous husband; exactly like I said. He was going to turn himself in!

- You need to show a little more professional courtesy Jorgensen. MgQuarck is being honoured with a full banquet and awards ceremony at the mayor's residence for his involvement in this case. Your conduct, on the other hand, is under review.

- I hate you MgQuarck.

- Squawk!

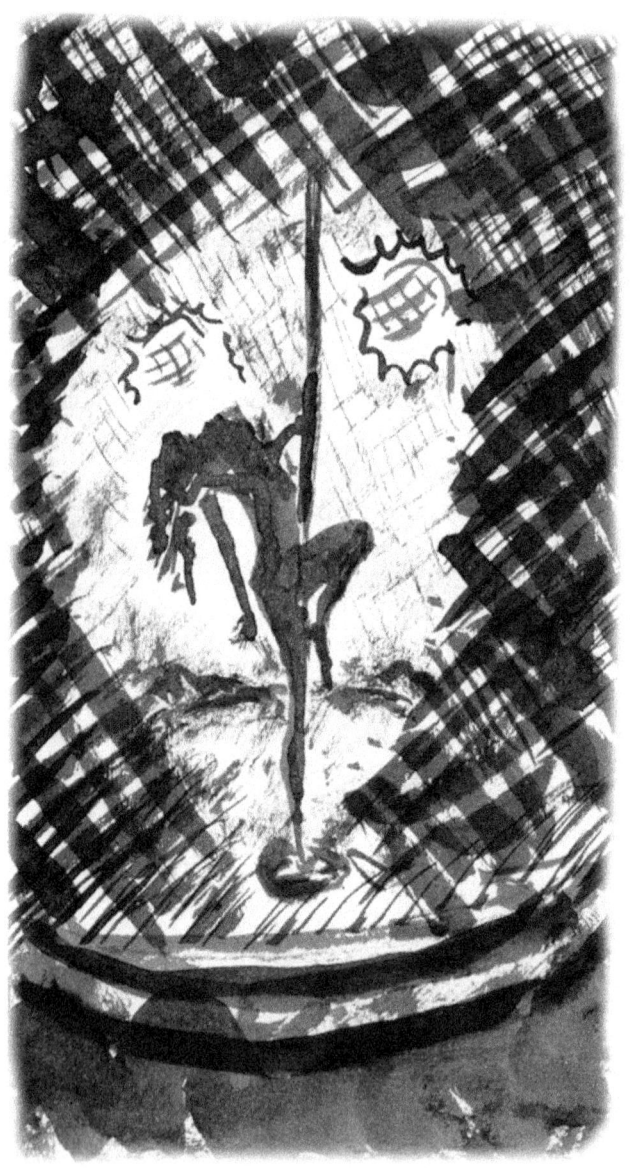

CHAPTER 2:

The Dangerous Beauty

of Victoria Falls

As a child, Victoria never dreamed of being a stripper.

As an adult, she entered the profession for practical reasons, born from financial necessity. She studied Business Economics at Leeds University but preferred cocaine and nightclubs to classrooms and notebooks so, when her marks dropped, her father refused to continue funding her bohemian lifestyle.

Victoria's father, Sir Reginald Lyon MacKenzie, christened her Elizabeth Windsor after the reigning monarch of the empire. She was born in Harare in February, 1977, the day of the silver jubilee. The youngest of six children, she moved with her family to

South Africa when Ian Smith, then prime-minister of Rhodesia, agreed to bi-racial rule. The family moved again, in 1994, to Manchester, three months before the election of Nelson Mandela and the ANC.

Victoria changed her name to suit her chosen vocation. Victoria Falls is the only place she could ever remember experiencing something resembling happiness.

Henri Viera is one of the few surviving members of *les Tirailleurs*, the legendary division of Senegalese soldiers in the French Army. When the unit officially disbanded in 1964 he moved to Bonaire, in the Dutch West Indies, and started a new life as a small businessman, operating an ambitious but discreet courier service between Columbia and the Florida Keys. Henri met Victoria at a nightclub in Miami.

To this day she has never met anybody faster in a fist fight and she has never seen him fire a gun. When she asked him why not he said the noise gave him migraines.

This was their final heist, after which, Victoria Falls would retire. Henri would be out of a job. He had an offer of employment, as head of security at her new club. She'd already made a down payment on a location in central Grande Prairie. It was perfect, for her. The joint would make a killing. In the winter she'd be close to her favourite ski resort and during the summers she would escape the hornets and the horseflies to visit Cuba, drink mojitos, and recruit new dancers.

She said communists make the finest spirits (and strippers) because they require them most. Victoria would be very happy.

Henri would not. The idea of winter in Grande Prairie made him think fondly of seven years in a Colombian prison. Henri did not know what he would do next. He didn't need to. Work always found him whether he liked it or not.

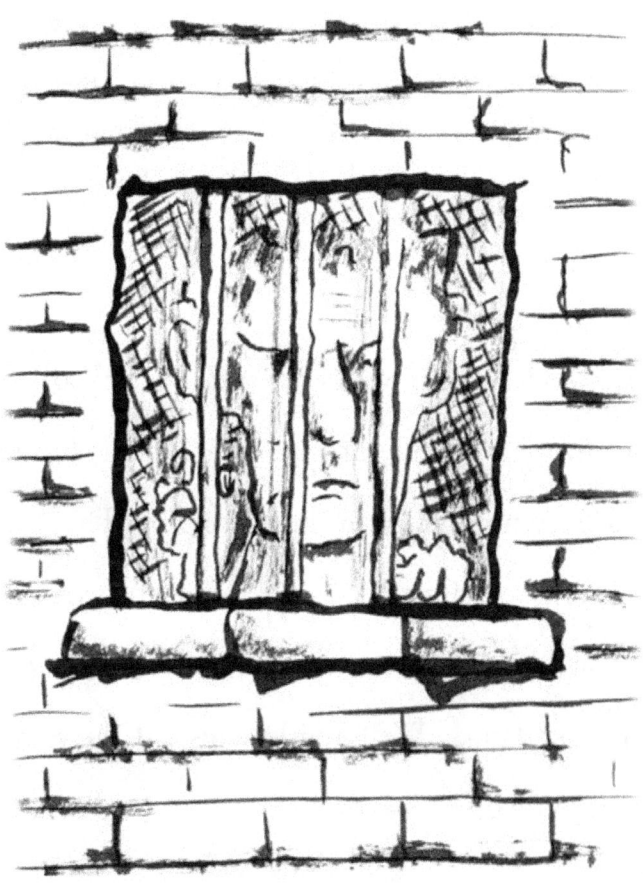

They had a lead on a construction boss delivering a bribe to a city official in exchange for a new contract on bridge maintenance and repairs. Henri needed only the time and place of the meeting. Victoria would discover the information and he would collect. This arrangement had been lucrative for them both for the previous dozen years but he was not unhappy to see the end. Very few people have the opportunity to walk away from the game in profit and out of prison.

- Henri, he's leaving now. Navy suit, black wool coat and a brown fedora. He drives a white Escalade and there's a Browning 9mm in the glove box. The meeting with the city clerk is in a mobile office trailer on a construction site, near the old airport. I only have one last dance. We'll rendezvous in Geneva next week and settle our accounts.

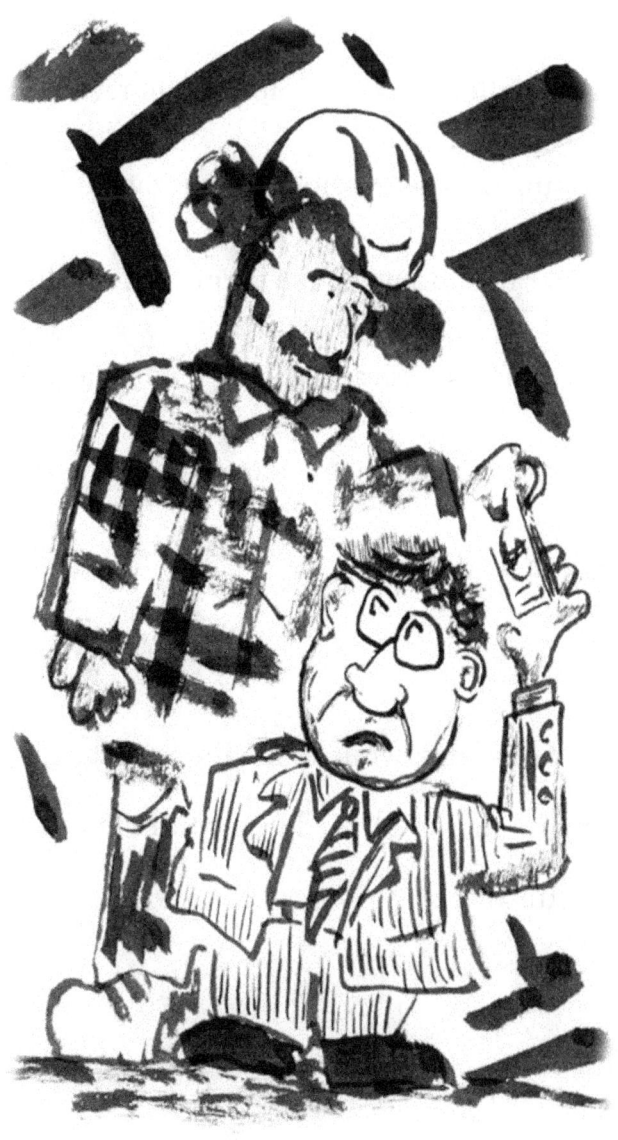

Victoria once told him about her surprise, every single time, by the volume of information revealed by men if gloating or boasting about money would encourage her to contravene the premises' guidelines regarding intimate physical contact. Henri merely shook his head. She did not understand men but, somehow, she used them.

Half-an-hour later, while removing her makeup in the dressing room, her phone lit up, with Henri's number on the display.

- Mlle. Victoria, *we have un probleme.* The two men are dead.

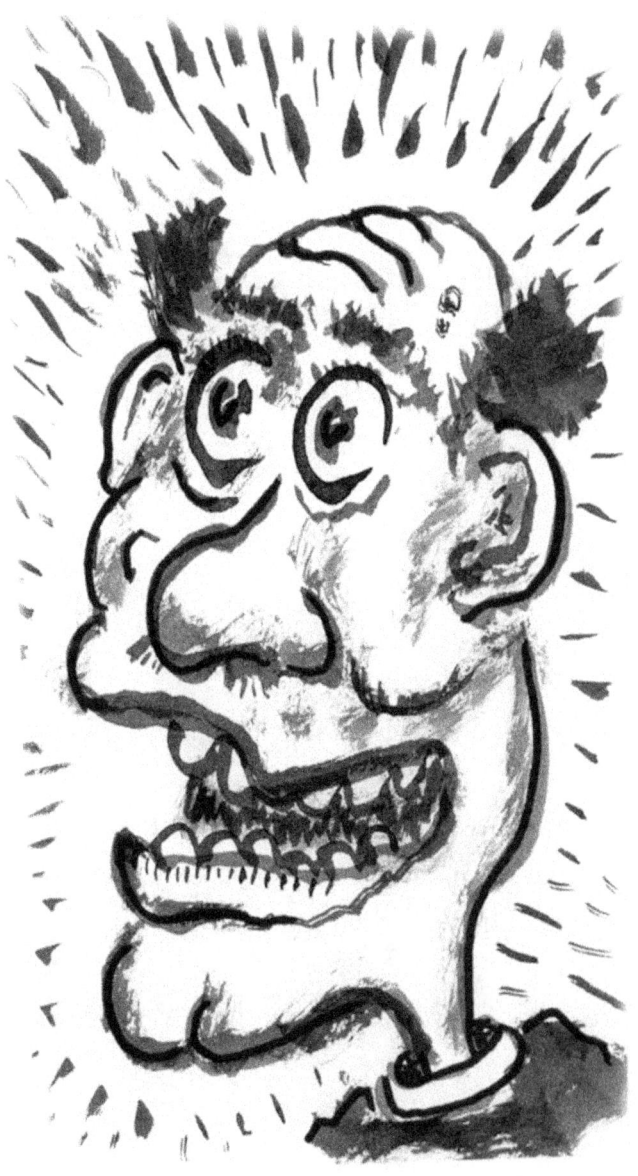

- Is the money still there?

-*Oui, Mlle. mais…*

- Quickly, grab the money and leave. If we follow the

plan there's no possibility they will link us with those

bodies.

- I cannot leave. There is an ostrich standing in the

corner wearing a trench coat and a pair of enormous

rubber boots. They are the biggest boots I have ever

seen. The ostrich is staring at me. I am very confused.

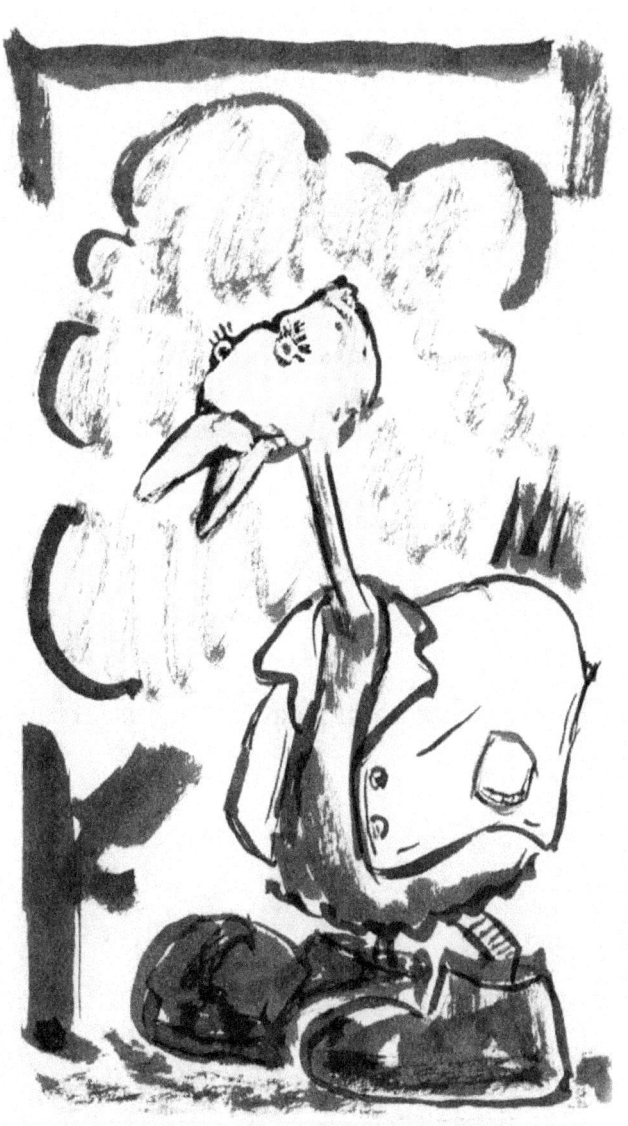

Victoria turned off her phone, removed the sim card and battery and dropped them both in a glass of water. She hurriedly started packing her bag. How did he know…?

- Ms. Falls, would you mind if we had a brief word?

Victoria did not turn around.

– Lt. Jorgensen, what an unpleasant surprise. How did you find me?

- Being honest ma'am, I've no idea. I hate that bird. You have the most disciplined operation I've ever

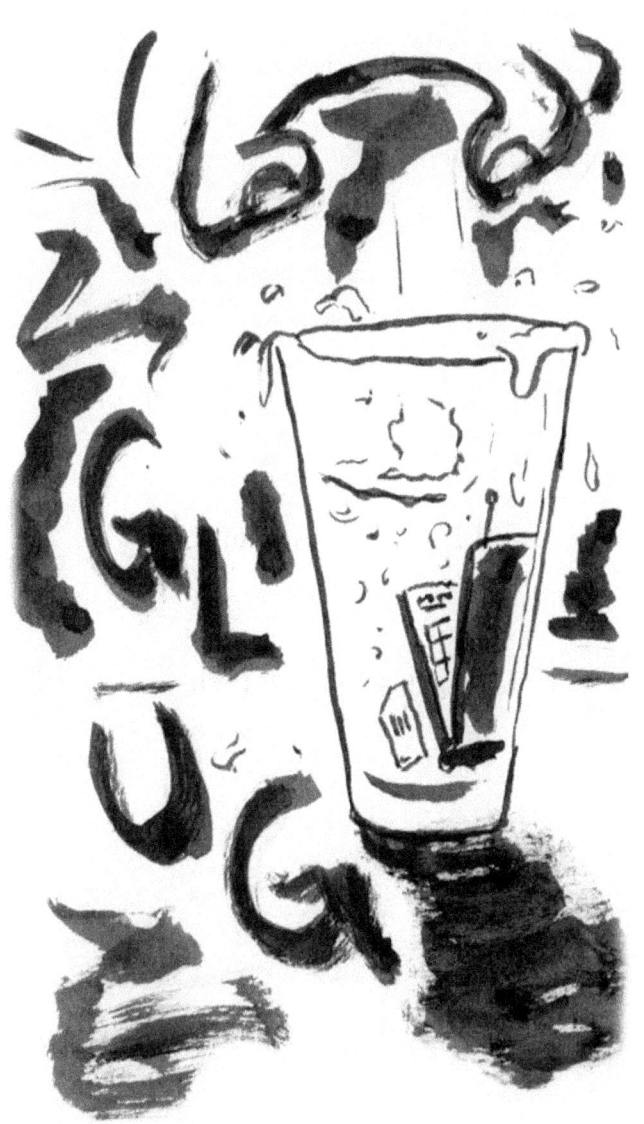

seen. Until last night our department didn't even know you were in the city. I haven't seen you since that one night in Denver…

- Don't ever mention Denver again. Doesn't it bother you? An escaped farm animal, doing your job?

- Sure does. I still have to arrest you.

- Of course you do, get on with it then…

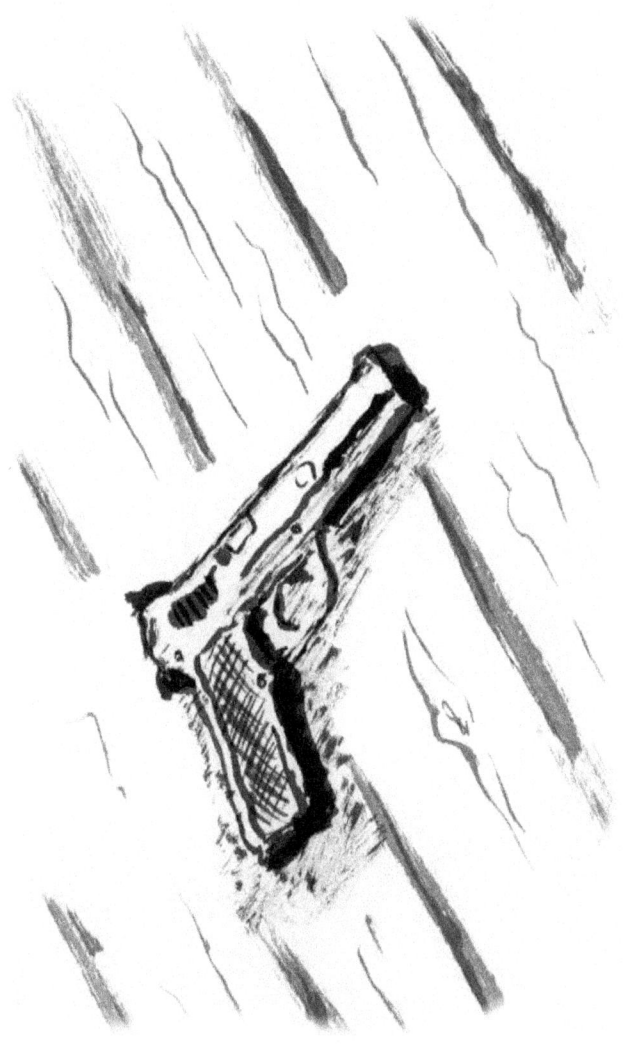

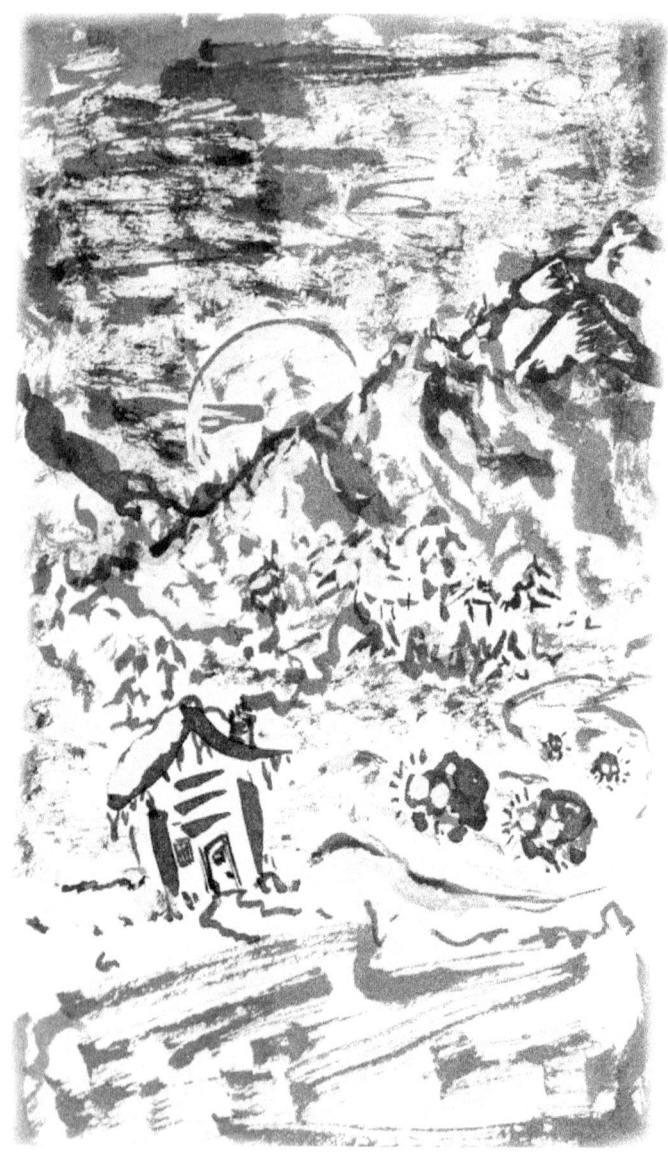

CHAPTER 3:

The Final Confession of Pierre Baudrillard

La vie, ce n'est pas facile.

I have travelled, I have sinned, I have been captured and I have escaped; but I have never before spoken about my job. I must hurry, they're closing fast. There are only a few minutes remaining until they arrive. Even now, I hear engines. There is no reason for any vehicles to be on this road, except to find me. I committed a most grievous violation for a man in my position. I broke an oral contract. My name is Pierre Baudrillard and I am an assassin.

I am an honourable man. I know the men in the black Escalades must find me. This is my story of why they must find me, the story of how I became the prey.

I was contracted to kill an exotic dancer. I never killed any women before but my new target was experienced and she knew the rules. She was clever - and elusive- but so are the men from whom she stole, and they do not call police. I tracked her across the continent. I caught up with her in the city I recently fled, and informed my employers. They arranged the bait. A man from their organisation would be in the club, drinking and talking loudly about his job. He would mention a meeting at the construction site. When she followed them I would kill her and dump the remains in the cement mixer. In the morning her body would be poured into the foundation of their new parking garage.

The first time I saw her dance I knew I would not do this. Instead I would kill the men, cut off their ears and present them to her, a trophy, as a symbol. A necklace of severed ears is guaranteed to win the heart of a beautiful woman. It is a more romantic gesture than the one by the great Dutch master, *M. Van Gogh*,

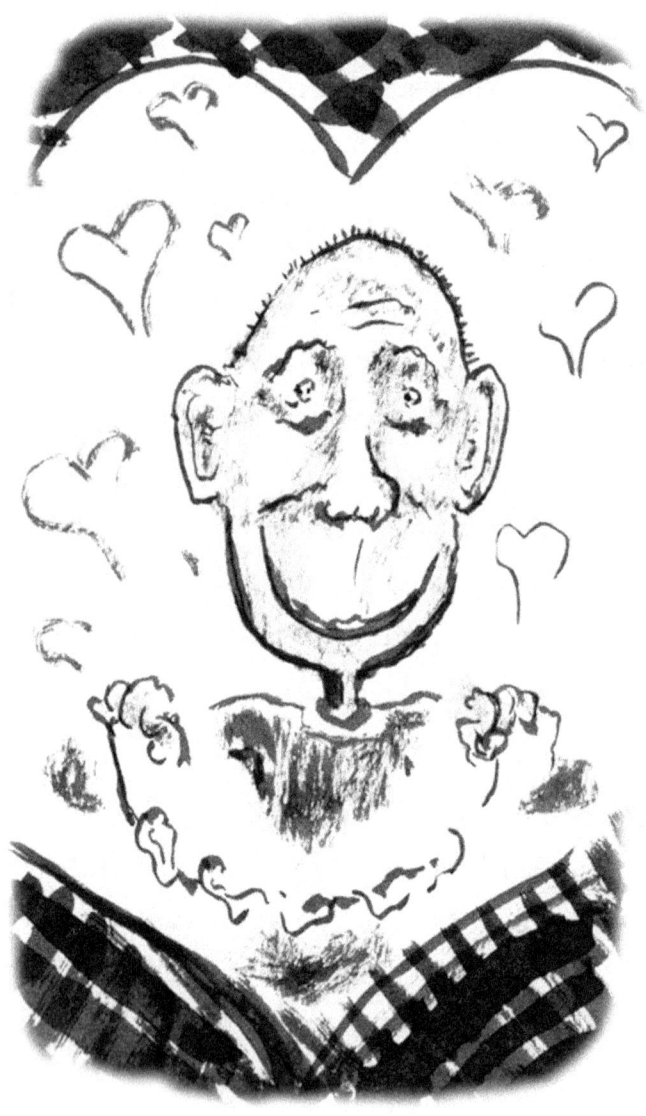

because he cut off his own ear. Obviously, a woman would find that to be weird.

In the mobile office trailer at the construction site, as I prepared to slice off *les oreilles* of the dead men, I saw a large black man approaching. Thinking the situation was beyond my control I rushed from the trailer to attack but ceased my attack almost as quickly when I saw the man's face in the light from the open door. It was Henri Viera. Thirty years ago we escaped, together, from a maximum security Colombian prison. I did not recognise him earlier when I saw him in the club, I was too busy watching the stage.

He came inside. I explained my situation and he explained his. He called his associate to inform her of the contract on her life. Just as he began speaking on the phone, an ostrich burst into the room, wearing the most enormous rubber boots I have ever seen.

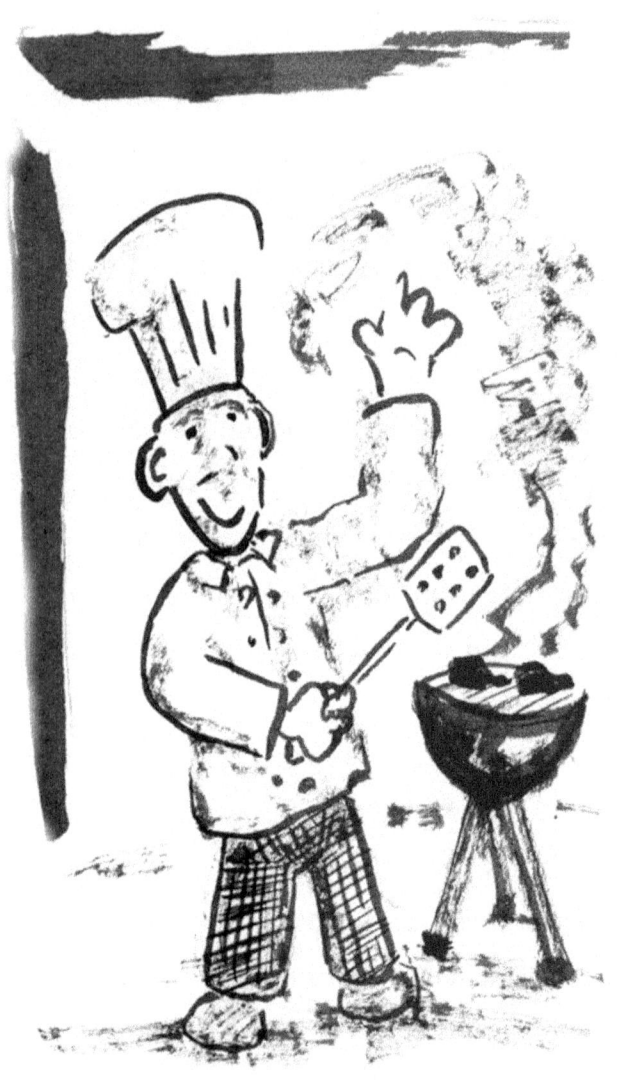

Henri, startled, expressed his confusion out loud. Then he stopped talking and looked at the phone. He had lost the connection.

I had not seen Henri for decades. We killed the ostrich, butchered and marinated some steaks, and stayed up all night, eating barbecue and drinking straight from the bottle of a rare Irish whiskey. (We found the whiskey in the bottom drawer of a filing cabinet, the same place we found the ostrich steak marinade. *C'est tellement bizarre.*)

The ostrich was the finest meal I'd ever eaten.

I cut off the ears of the dead men, to keep for myself. I knew then, *je pourrais jamais gagne la coeur de mon amour.* Henri and I parted ways and now, I find myself here.

They have nearly caught me. Perhaps it is time I should be the predator once more?

merci, bonne santé.

Epilogue:

Revenge of the Cassowary

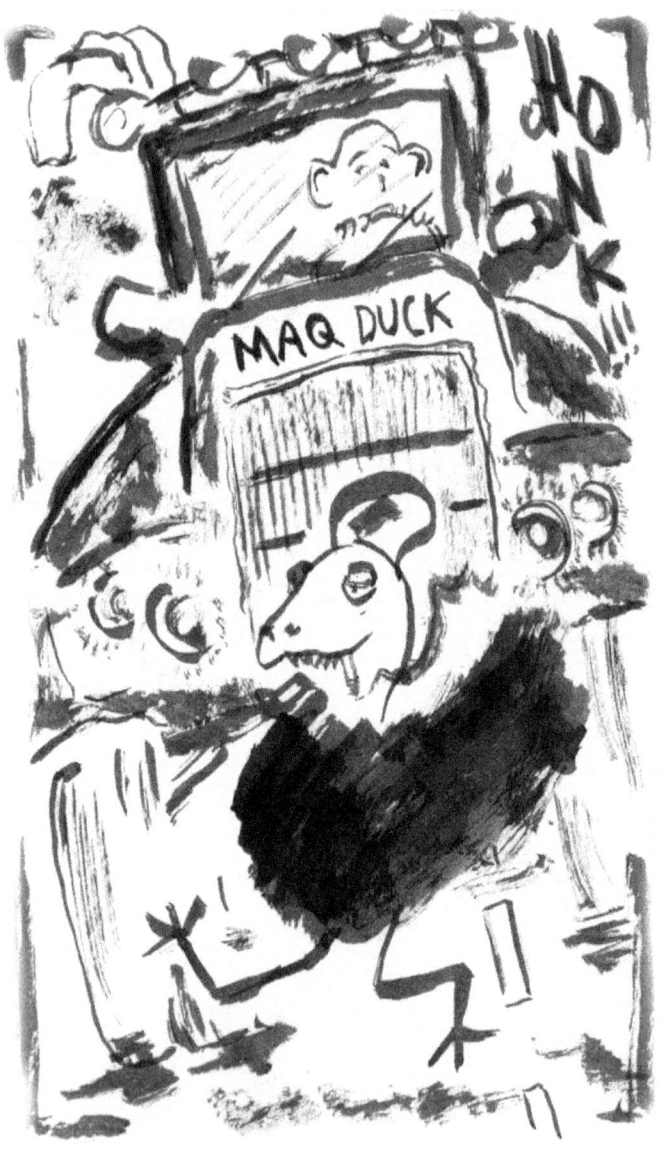

-Good night chief, have a great weekend.

-Thank you sergeant. Say hi to your wife for me.

-Nothing doing chief. Oh, and chief?

-Yes sergeant?

-Stay off the freeway on your way home, there's an escaped cassowary on the road. It's caused a massive traffic jam near the 97 street exits.

-Dear god! Why didn't anyone tell me? Is Jorgensen still here?

-Yes chief.

-Send him in immediately. We have precious little time.

-You wanted to see me chief?

-Jorgensen, there's not a moment to lose. The Cassowary has escaped.

-What's that sir?

-The Cassowary, crime kingpin of Queensland. He's flown the coop and flapping havoc on the freeway. Who knows what crackpot caper is lurking in his criminal mind.

-(aw crap)

-Get moving Jorgensen!

-Sir, isn't this a job better suited to animal control?

-This is too big for animal control. This might be too big for us all. The Cassowary is the dastardly mastermind behind the Great Train Robbery near London in '63.

-er...that was Bruce Richard Reynolds, sir.

-Was it? Oh, well he was certainly behind the recent theft of the Mona Lisa.

-The Mona Lisa was last stolen in 1911 by Vincenzo Peruggia. He was caught and arrested in 1913 and the painting was returned to the Louvre. It's still there.

-I heard that one's a fake, forged by the Cassowary himself.

-Where'd you hear that chief?

-On the internets...

-Chief, what did I tell you about drinking and reading the internet? Listen, for the last time, flightless birds are not detectives or criminals, they are zoo animals.

Or they is food.

-Bite your tongue Jorgensen, you bite your tongue. To speak so ill of the dead, the great Ostrich MgQuarck still warm in his grave.

-Warm in the toilet bowl you mean, because they killed him then cooked him and ate him. That's what happens to a dead ostrich chief, they're exceptionally delicious.

-Be quiet Jorgenson, I order you to be quiet. Anyways, the Cassowary is still alive, and dangerous.

-Of course cassowaries are dangerous sir, they are giant, fast-moving flightless birds with razor sharp claws and a temper. Fortunately, they have the brains of a cassowary. Once animal control gets hold of him the problem is solved.

-This is your case Jorgenson, I suggest you step lively if you value your job.

-I hate my job.

-What's that Jorgensen?

-Nothing sir.

-Case closed chief. We have a truck driver in custody. One Peter Bonduran, aka Pierre Baudrillard, the notorious Irish assassin from Trois Rivieres. He used to speak with the most outrageously fake French accent. He's wanted across North America for a string of murders and robberies, including the recent massacre of three dozen well known mafia hitmen at a remote log cabin near Hinton.

-What about the cassowary?

-The cassowary is dead sir. Bonduran shot him. He's been charged with illegally discharging a firearm within city limits.

-God bless that leprechaun Jorgenson, God bless them all.

-Don't use the "L" word chief, it make them... angry...

-Angry? Leprechauns?

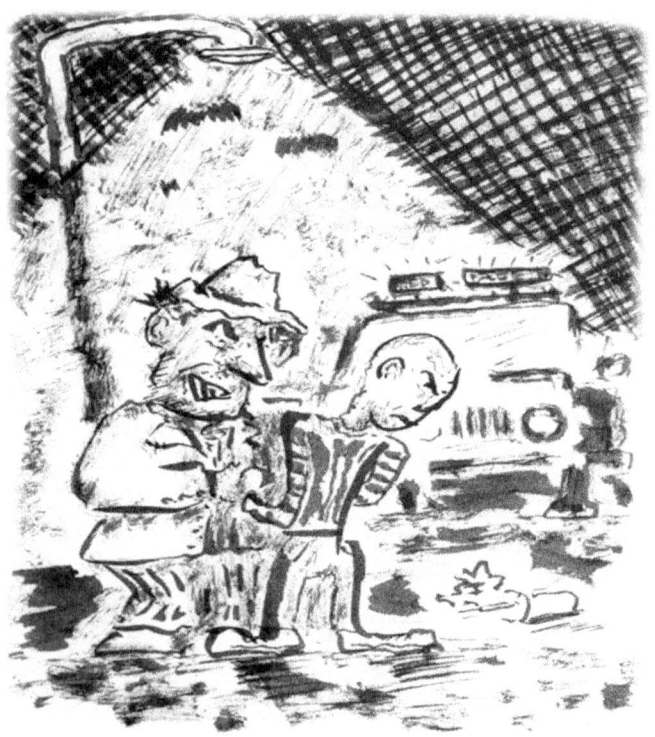

Definitely the End

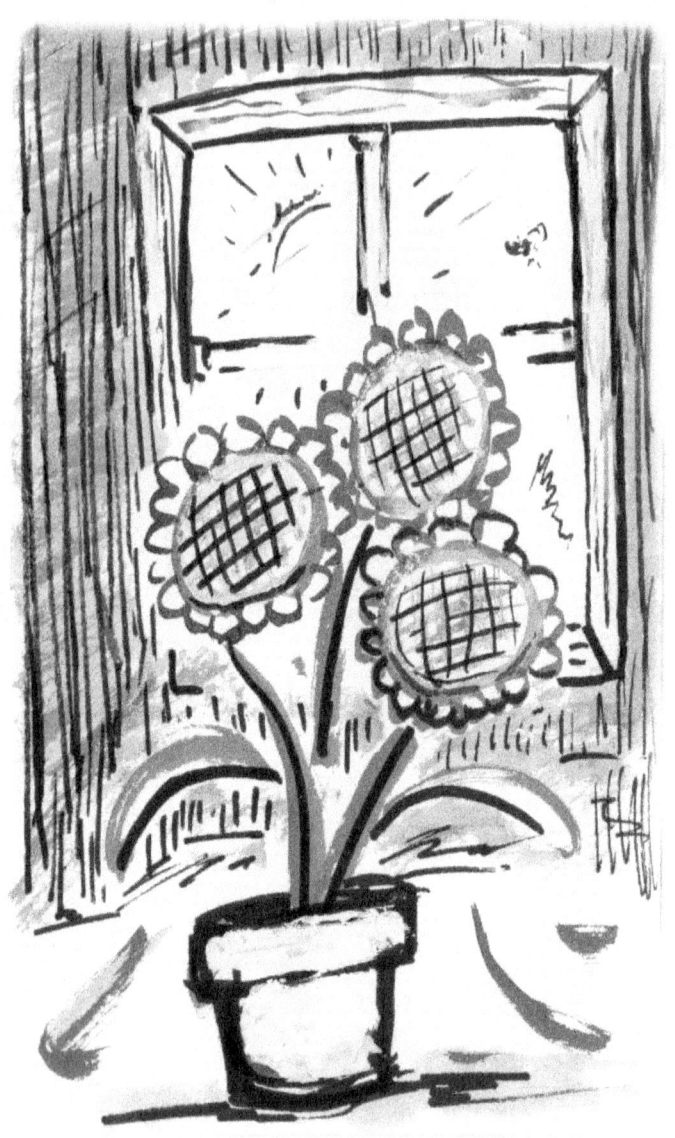

www.ingramcontent.com/pod-product-compliance
Lightning Source LLC
Chambersburg PA
CBHW061221180526
45170CB00003B/1103